I LOVE CORN

Copyright © 2023 Brad Gosse

I have over 100 humor books and several strange coloring books available on Amazon.

My humor books cover a wide range of topics and styles, from dumb jokes and puns to satirical takes on current events. Whatever your sense of humor, you'll find something to love or hate in my collection.

And for those who want to tap into their creative side, my strange coloring books offer unique and unconventional designs for you to color in and make your own. These books are perfect for relaxing after a long day, or for getting in touch with your inner artist.

So don't wait any longer to add some laughter and creativity to your life. Check out my other books on Amazon today!

Here are just a few...

books.bradgosse.com

IN THE LAND OF CORN
I'M A CONNOISSEUR

FROM CORN HOLE TO CREAM CORN
I'M ALWAYS SURE

MEET MY STEPMOM
HER CORN'S OUTTA SIGHT

SHE LOVES IT SO MUCH
IT'S HER FAVOURITE DELIGHT

BUT SHE CHOKES AND SHE GAGS
IT'S QUITE A DISPLAY

I THOUGHT IT WAS THE KERNELS
BUT SHE LIKES IT THAT WAY

THE WOMEN IN CORN
WORK DAY AND NIGHT

THEIR CORN CREATIONS
A TASTY DELIGHT

MY FAVORITE CORN SQUIRTS
OH IT'S A THRILL

LIKE A CORN VOLCANO
THAT'S ABOUT TO SPILL

STEPSISTER AND FRIENDS
THEY'RE IN ON THE GAME

STUCK BY THAT CORN GLUE
IT'S ALWAYS THE SAME

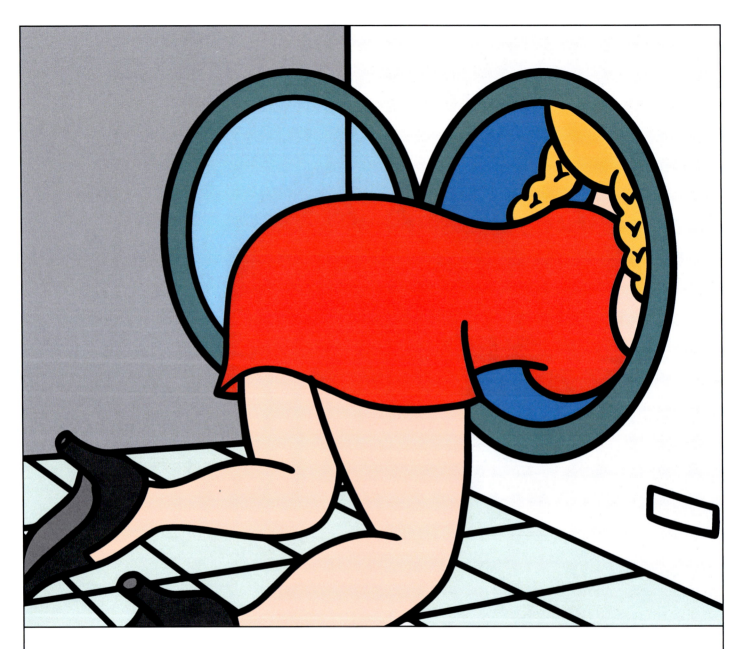

BUT WHEN IT GETS STICKY
I LEND A HAND TOO

WE HELP EACH OTHER
YO, THAT'S WHAT WE DO

WHEN I'M ALL ALONE
MY CORN LOVE IS FREE

NO ONE WATCHES ME
WATCH MY CORNOGRAPHY

I COVER MY TRACKS
YO MY SECRET'S WELL-KEPT

FOR MY LOVE OF CORN
YOU CAN CALL ME ADEPT

BLACK CORN, AND WHITE CORN
DELICIOUS, IT'S TRUE

RED, BLUE, YELLOW CORN
WHAT ABOUT YOU?

I'M ADDICTED, I CONFESS
IT'S BECOME THE NORM

BUT HERE, AT WORK
I CAN NO LONGER PERFORM

HR SAT ME DOWN, "TAKE A VACATION, MY FRIEND...

...NO MORE CORN AT THE OFFICE
THIS HAS TO END."

NOW MY WORK IS CORN-FREE
IT'S A SAD REFORM

BUT NOW I'M AT HOME AND
I WEATHER THE STORM

MY FAMILY'S CONCERNED
THEY'VE LEFT ME ALONE

CORN HABIT'S SO WILD
I GOT MY OWN TIME ZONE

CORN'S MORE THAN FOOD
IT'S MY LIFETIME PLAN

IF I COULD, I'D TURN THIS WHOLE WORLD TO CORNLAND

MIKE HUNT
SMELLS LIKE FISH

Clap along with Mike Hunt. This book is filled with hilarious double entendres. You know what it's about. Don't make me spell it out for you. This book is cheap as balls. Like your mom.

MIKE LIT
Shouldn't Be Hard To Find

Every girl, and some guys want my big black hawk. This book teaches you why big black hawks matter.

ALL THE GIRLS LOVE
MY BIG BLACK HAWK

CUCUMBER CURTIS

Can't come to dinner. Your mom has other plans for this innocent little vegetable.

GLUCK GLUCK 3000

Sex Robots are the new wave of the future in sexual entertainment. In fact, they're already in the process of being built. Catering to the needs of lonely men and women, these bots will soon be ubiquitous.

RACE WARS

Black, car, white car, and yellow car too.

STD'S & YOU

Learning From The Animals At The Zoo

CONJOINED TWINS
Where Does One End and The Other Begin?

What if one can swim and the other can not? Can just one of them become an astronaut? How often do they need a diaper change? If they grew 100 feet tall wouldn't that be strange? Are they a by-product of nuclear radiation? Have they ever been left outside a fire station?

...UT INBREEDING WITH ...KEYBEAR

...usins or ...will

...learn ...ear. He's hearing about it for the first time.

MOM RUNS TRAINS
On The Weekend With Dad's Friends

Career Day

It's career day at school. And I get to present. I'm so proud of my mom. And the weekends she's spent. Learning to run trains.

SANTAS LIL HUMPER
SAVES CHRISTMAS

Santa crashes in the Middle East and Rudolf is dead. Only a strange camel can save Christmas now.

BAA BAA BLACK SHEEP
Deals With Another Routine Stop

Baa baa black sheep please step out of the car. Yes sir yes sir please know I'm unarmed. Do you know why I stopped you today?. "Because of the fur color I display?". You match the description of a suspect I seek. Funny it's the 4th time to happen this week. I profiled you because you are black. And you drive a Mercedes which seems kinda whack.

Brad Gosse

MOMS O...
New Beginnings From Difficult Choices

Dad left your mom broke. Now she's faced with the harsh reality of not having enough money. But don't worry she has a plan to get back on her feet.

CLIP CLOP
The Racist Horse Cop

Does Anyone Know Whatever Happened To
MURDER HORNETS

Remember Murder Hornets? Whatever happened to them? We dive deeply into the terror phenomenon that never came to be. 2020 had so many bigger things, so Murder Hornets were forgotten.

Make Your Own Luck

What can pimps and divorce lawyers teach children, about money and luck? This book tells the story of outdated wisdom and harsh truths.

Cockroach-baby smells really musky. Centipede baby was sewn from human skin. Squid-fish lives deep down in the sea. Flesh-eating ladybug is super scary. Bearded baby was born this hairy.

CREEPY CREATURES
KEEPING YOU AWAKE WITH QUESTIONS

SOFA KING

KLUKEE
The Plant Based Chicken

OURS BABY
The Only Child Your Step Mom Loves

Your stepmom wants one thing from your dear old dad. Viable sperm and an empty house. Pack your bags it's time to grow up.

MOMMY GOT A DUI

Your mom has secrets. She hides her drinking from you… Until now. Mommy can't drive you to school and you're going to have to learn the bus routes.

INSOMNIAC & FRIENDS
The Clowns That Put You To Sleep

Yeetyeet likes to watch you sleep. Pickles under your bed he creeps. Switchblade eats your favorite stuffies. Pedo lures you away with puppies. Shifty plans to collect your teeth. Twisty smells your hair while you sleep. Clammy lives inside his van. Hank once had to kill a man. Tooty smells your dirty socks. Busby laughs at electric shocks. Twinkles spends the night robbing graves. Fappy keeps a few human slaves.

MY RACIST GRAN

WHY DADDY HITS MOMMY

A Kids Guide To Understanding Alcoholism

DEAD BABIES
COLORING BOOKS

TRIGGERED
Kids Guide To Cancel Culture

Easily offended is the new trend. People act outraged. Be careful, you might lose your job. Even though nobody is responsible for the feelings of others.

OK BOOMER

Boomer always complains at the store. But it was on sale yesterday!! When yesterday's special isn't available anymore. You shouldn't be such a slut. Boomer gives unsolicited advice. This smart phone is dumber than dirt. Boomer always struggles with his device. Boomer demands your supervisor.

CANDIS NUTS
Come In The Morning Each Day

MELT IN YOUR MOUTH

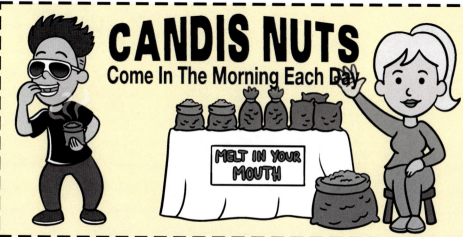

CINNAMON

A horse forced into the sex trade.

Brad Gosse

DON'T BATHE WITH UNCLE JOE
Setting Boundaries With Adults

Uncle Joe lost his job. For misconduct in the workplace. He's coming to stay with us. You're going to have to learn to avoid his hands and more importantly. NEVER bathe with uncle Joe.

THIRST TRAPS
Why Moms Phone Keeps Blowing Up

DADDY'S A SIMP
Don't Expect Much Inheritance

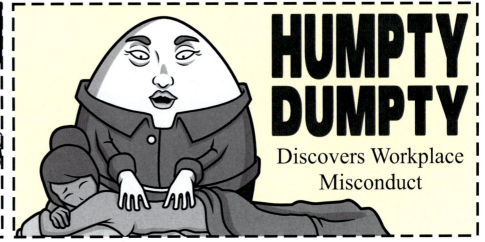

HUMPTY DUMPTY
Discovers Workplace Misconduct

Made in United States
Orlando, FL
18 September 2023

37047535R00024